Shropshire's Lost Railway

by David James

Cambrian Railways No. 15 at Llanymynech.

1

Text © David James
First Published in the United Kingdom, 2006
Stenlake Publishing Limited
54–58 Mill Square, Catrine
KA5 6RD
www.stenlake.co.uk

ISBN 9781840333848

Printed by Blissetts, Roslin Road, Acton, W3 8DH

The publishers regret that they cannot supply copies of any pictures featured in this book.

Picture Acknowledgements

The publishers wish to thank the following for contributing photographs to this book: John Alsop for the inside front cover and pages 1, 2, 6-11, 13-28, 29 (both), 30-33, 36-38, 41, 42 ,43 (both), 45-48 the inside back cover and the back cover; and Richard Casserley for pages 4, 5, 12, 34, 35, 39 and 44.

Condover Station.

INTRODUCTION

The history of Britain's modern railways began back in the 1820s with the opening for freight traffic of the Stockton to Darlington Railway. This was followed by the more famous Liverpool to Manchester line of 1830, the first to provide a regular passenger timetable. The success of this latter route led to the development of numerous other adjoining lines, and by the 1840s Britain was gripped by a 'Railway Mania' as companies proposing new railways sprang up throughout the country.

Despite its ancient Marcher lands along the English-Welsh border, connections to the neighbouring counties of Cheshire, Staffordshire, Worcestershire and Herefordshire (where railway lines had already been built or were planned), and its relative proximity to the rapidly industrialising West Midlands, the county of Shropshire had to wait until late 1848 before the first locomotive-hauled trains reached its county capital at Shrewsbury thanks to the appropriately named Shrewsbury & Chester Railway. This event sparked further development, with the Shrewsbury & Birmingham Railway opening a line from Shrewsbury via Wellington to Oakengates and hence on to Wolverhampton and beyond during 1849, followed by the Shropshire Union company adding a link across the county boundary to Stafford. Then, during 1853, the Shrewsbury & Hereford Railway built a line through the southern regions of Shropshire from Shrewsbury to Ludlow and thence on in to Herefordshire to complete the picture.

From these basic arteries of main-line links several smaller branches soon began to grow, with the Shrewsbury & Chester again leading the way as early as 1848 by completing a short line between Oswestry and Gobowen. Other companies and lines followed to connect with some of Shropshire's more isolated towns and villages, although for most of these routes the transporting of fare-paying passengers was a secondary consideration compared to the movement of freight, especially minerals, stone or agricultural produce. Also, despite being one of England's most rural counties, Shropshire could additionally lay claim to being the birthplace of Britain's industrial revolution for it was here, around the village of Coalbrookdale, that Abraham Darby honed his methods of producing superior quality ironwork using coke to fire his furnaces instead of traditional charcoal. As a result, by the late 1700s this corner of Shropshire had evolved into a hive of industry with myriad coal mines, furnaces, ironworks and other factories. Supplying these and transporting away their finished goods became a major goal of various local branches.

The Shrewsbury & Birmingham, Shrewsbury & Chester and Shrewsbury & Hereford eventually became known as 'The Fighting Shrewsburys' as they became the focal points of a struggle for control between the London & North Western Railway and its main rival within Shropshire, the Great Western Railway. The clash between these two giants led to both the Shrewsbury & Birmingham and Shrewsbury & Chester eventually falling under the control of the Great Western during 1854. Meanwhile, jurisdiction over the Shrewsbury & Hereford was finally settled when the London & North Western and the Great Western agreed to run it as a joint concern. This enabled the Shrewsbury & Hereford's line to become part of a much larger chain from north-west England to South Wales and the West Country. This enlarged through route increased in importance once the famous Severn Tunnel opened in 1886.

Links across the frontier into Wales were also inevitable and by the 1860s the Cambrian Railways company had established its headquarters at Oswestry, turning this once small market town into an important railway centre, while other railway firms from the neighbouring counties of Cheshire and Staffordshire (such as the North Staffordshire Railway) also grabbed tentative footholds in parts of Shropshire.

Shropshire's assortment of rural branches suffered a handful of early demises simply because they were too uneconomical to be justified and passenger numbers across a great many more lines always remained low. Some branches managed to struggle on into the 1920s or 30s, but growth in road transportation was blamed for the closure of a number of lines from that time on. This became indisputable after the Second World War when improved bus connections, an increase in private car ownership and developments in lorry design, combined with a considerable road-building programme, killed off even more routes. Those that somehow survived this blow then had their numbers culled even further by the infamous Beeching cutbacks of the early 1960s.

As a consequence the rail network across Shropshire today is but a pale and feeble shadow of its former glory. Most of what remains is basically the old 'Fighting Shrewsburys' main lines, which have been downgraded in importance to secondary status. The multitude of small branches was all but swept away and it is to these 'lost' lines that this book will address its attention. The reader should note that I have defined Shropshire as it exists today following the 1974 local government boundary reorganisation and so have tried to concentrate coverage on those lines that existed wholly within Shropshire's borders. However some divergence is necessary in places, especially when referring to routes operated by the likes of the Cambrian Railways. It should also be noted that I have listed all lines in chronological order according to their opening dates

Oswestry—Gobowen Branch

Passenger service withdrawn	7 November 1966
Distance	2 miles
Company	Shrewsbury & Chester Railway

Stations closed	*Date*
Oswestry *	7 July 1924
Park Hall Halt	7 November 1966

* The original station closed in 1866 and was replaced by a new GWR facility. Trains were later diverted to Oswestry (Cam) after July 1924.

Oswestry Station, June 1956.

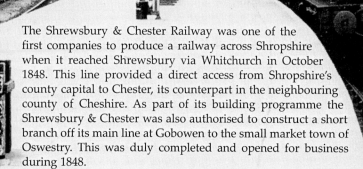

The Shrewsbury & Chester Railway was one of the first companies to produce a railway across Shropshire when it reached Shrewsbury via Whitchurch in October 1848. This line provided a direct access from Shropshire's county capital to Chester, its counterpart in the neighbouring county of Cheshire. As part of its building programme the Shrewsbury & Chester was also authorised to construct a short branch off its main line at Gobowen to the small market town of Oswestry. This was duly completed and opened for business during 1848.

Oswestry Station, September 1958, facing Whitchurch.

The branch had only one intermediate stop at Park Hall and passenger services arriving at Oswestry terminated at the town's Shrewsbury & Chester station. For a dozen years this remained Oswestry's only railway station until a line to Welshpool was opened by the Cambrian Railways. By then the Shrewsbury & Chester had passed into history after being absorbed by the Great Western Railway six years earlier. Following that firm's takeover of the Cambrian Railways as a result of the Groupings of 1923, the original Shrewsbury & Chester station at Oswestry was closed and trains heading to or from Gobowen were switched to the former Cambrian complex.

Despite its short length the branch did moderately well for itself. For example, during both the First and Second World Wars the line's halt at Park Hall became a focus for military activity as a transit camp was built nearby for troops heading overseas. A shuttle service between Gobowen and Oswestry also became popular with the local community.

In fact, despite increasing road competition, the branch managed to hold its own for two years longer than the nearby (and longer) Oswestry to Welshpool link. But ultimately the greater convenience and lower operating costs of the surrounding road network, coupled with the nationalised British Railways' need to implement radical cuts in the wake of the notorious Beeching Report meant that the line had to close. The final passenger train for Gobowen therefore left Oswestry on 7 November 1966.

Wellington—Newport—Stafford

Passenger service withdrawn	7 September 1964	Stations closed		Date
Distance	18 miles	Donnington *		7 September 1964
Company	Shropshire Union Railways & Canal Company	Newport (Salop) **		7 September 1964

Stations closed	Date
Hadley	7 September 1964
Trench Crossing	7 September 1964

* First opened as Donnington before being renamed Donnington Wood in January 1871. The original name was restored in July 1871.

** Originally known as Newport.

Trench Crossing Station, mid 1920s.

Once the Shrewsbury & Birmingham Railway had proposed and obtained Parliamentary approval for a line from Shrewsbury to Birmingham other schemes were quickly promoted to connect with it. One of these was sponsored by the Shropshire Union Railways & Canal Company which suggested a railway from Wellington on the Shrewsbury & Birmingham's line to Stafford, the county capital of neighbouring Staffordshire. From there travellers from Shropshire would be able to change trains and travel over London & North Western Railway metals to London, Manchester or Liverpool.

Donnington Station, late 1920s.

The Shropshire Union Railways & Canal Company was itself the creation of a merger between the Shrewsbury and Shropshire Union Canal companies to which the nearby Montgomeryshire Canal was later added. This newly unified organisation recognised the threat posed to Britain's existing canal system by the emergence of the railways and it sought to protect itself by developing its own rail links (often by converting defunct canals into trackways). As the saying goes 'keep your friends close but your enemies closer' - by embracing the railways that was just what the Shropshire Union Railways & Canal Company was doing.

The company though soon found itself embroiled in the rivalry between the Great Western Railway and the London & North Western. This pressure culminated in the Shropshire Union Railways & Canal Company eventually being leased to the London & North Western in 1847, not long after it had won Parliament's approval for its planned Wellington—Stafford link.

Despite the London & North Western's takeover, the projected line went ahead and opened for business on 1 June 1849 - the same day as trains began running between Shrewsbury and Oakengates on the Shrewsbury & Birmingham Railway. At first the Shropshire Union Railways & Canal Company was the only means for passengers from Shrewsbury to reach London by train, though the fares levied for such lengthy journeys were far from cheap and so deterred many from using the service.

At Shrewsbury trains for Stafford commenced from the town's single station, close to the remains of a medieval castle by the River Severn. This facility, designed by the Chester architect and railway engineer T.M. Penson, was served not just by the Shropshire Union Railways & Canal Company but also the pioneering Shrewsbury & Chester Railway and the Shrewsbury & Birmingham, so it was soon busy with trains coming and going in several directions.

After holding an unchallenged position for five years the Shropshire Union Railways & Canal Company's status as the only rail link to London from Shropshire was broken by the much-delayed opening of the Shrewsbury & Birmingham's line as far as Birmingham, from where other routes to the capital were available. This offered a journey distance of just 30 miles to Birmingham direct from Shrewsbury instead of 46 miles (with a change at Stafford) via the Shropshire Union Railways & Canal Company. As a result increasing numbers of passengers switched to the shorter route and in a desperate bid to attract them back the Shropshire Union Railways & Canal Company launched a massive price war against the S&B. At one point the company charged travellers just a penny per 10 miles.

Newport (Salop) Station, early 1920s.

This strategy worked and heavy discounting enabled the Shropshire Union Railways & Canal Company's line to remain open. However, its profits were never high and so it was always vulnerable to economic downturns and competition from alternative modes of transport. Indeed, during the line's later years fewer and fewer people actually travelled along its entirety with most using it only to reach Newport.

The Shropshire Union Railways & Canal Company was formally absorbed by the London & North Western during 1922 and following the Grouping the next year that company itself became part of the London, Midland & Scottish Railway. The same period also saw the widespread advent of regular local bus services and an increase in private car ownership. Against these two menaces the branch could do little and its passenger numbers dropped sharply.

Somehow it struggled on through the Second World War and into the era of the nationalised British Railways. However, the Beeching Report signalled the death knell. Passenger trains were officially withdrawn in September 1964, although freight continued to use the line between Donnington and Newport and then into Staffordshire until 1966 when services were cut back to work between the two Shropshire sites only. This lasted for three more years and thereafter the line was only in use to allow access to a short 2-mile spur of track leading to a military stores depot near Donnington. This eventually closed in July 1991, bringing the line's usefulness to an end.

The Coalbrookdale Branch

Passenger service withdrawn	21 September 1925
Distance	5 miles
Company	Shrewsbury & Birmingham Railway

Stations closed	*Date*
Madeley (Salop) *	21 September 1925
Lightmoor Halt **	23 July 1962
Coalbrookdale ***	23 July 1962

* Originally known as Madeley between June 1854 and October 1884, before becoming Madeley Court from October 1884 until June 1897. The station was closed between March 1915 and July 1925.

** Originally known as Lightmoor between June 1854 and November 1864 before closing. It reopened as Lightmoor Platform in August 1907 but closed again between January 1917 and July 1919. It was renamed as Lightmoor Halt in February 1956.

*** Reopened and renamed as Telford (Coalbrookdale) in May 1979. It became Ironbridge Gorge in July 1988 and as such remains open.

Lightmoor Halt.

Around 1767 cast-iron rails began to be produced locally in south Shropshire by the likes of the Coalbrookdale Company. These were often laid to replace elderly wooden rails which provided a trackway for the movement of goods from Coalbrookdale to the ironworks at Horsehay, roughly 2 miles to the north. This whole area was rich in iron foundries and coal mines and was later to become famous for producing the very first cast-iron cylinders employed on early steam engines.

By 1847 the industries around Coalbrookdale had grown to such an extent that the Shrewsbury & Birmingham Railway obtained permission to link the area with its own main line at Madeley Junction near Shifnal. On 1 June 1854 this 5-mile-long, freight-dominated line opened for business as far as Lightmoor, with an intermediate stop at Madeley.

Coalbrookdale Station, early 1920s.

Three months later the line passed into the hands of the Great Western Railway following its takeover of the Shrewsbury & Birmingham. After a decade of Great Western operations the company took the decision to extend the line a further mile from Lightmoor to connect with Coalbrookdale, itself already connected to the rail network by the Much Wenlock & Severn Junction Railway (which was reliant upon the Great Western for its trains).

The Great Western's station at Coalbrookdale opened in November 1864 and a limited through-passenger service to Shifnal and beyond along the former Shrewsbury & Birmingham main line was devised. However, customer numbers were never high and the entire branch remained heavily freight orientated throughout its working life. It was little surprise therefore when the Great Western withdrew passenger trains in 1915. An experimental two-month revival followed in the summer of 1925 but this too was judged a failure.

A portion of the branch between Lightmoor and Coalbrookdale remained open for passenger trains though as part of the more successful Severn Junction line until the 1960s (see that line's entry for details). Also, the section from Madeley to Shifnal remained in use for goods and parcels traffic for several more years with the emphasis gradually switching to the transporting of coal from the nearby mines. Such traffic continues today over this stretch of line, with merry-go-round trains traversing it as they continually feed the modern power station at Ironbridge.

Wellington—Craven Arms (including the Severn Junction Line)

Passenger service withdrawn	23 July 1962
Distance	28 miles
Companies	Wellington & Severn Junction Railway/
	Much Wenlock & Severn Junction Railway/
	Much Wenlock, Craven Arms & Coalbrookdale Railway

Stations closed	*Date*
Ketley	23 July 1962
Ketley Town Halt	23 July 1962
New Dale Halt	23 July 1962
Lawley Bank	23 July 1962
Horsehay & Dawley *	23 July 1962
Doseley Halt	23 July 1962
Lightmoor Halt **	23 July 1962
Green Bank Halt	23 July 1962
Coalbrookdale **	23 July 1962
Farley Halt	23 July 1962

Stations closed	*Date*
Much Wenlock ***	23 July 1962
Stretton Westwood Crossing	31 December 1951
Westwood Halt	31 December 1951
Presthope	31 December 1951
Easthope Halt	31 December 1951
Longville	31 December 1951
Rushbury	31 December 1951
Harton Road	31 December 1951
Wistanstow Halt	11 June 1956
Stretford Bridge Junction ****	20 April 1935

* Originally known as Horsehay.
** See previous entry for details.
*** Original station closed in August 1884 and was replaced by a new building.
**** First closed briefly in 1877 before reopening in July of the same year.

Horsehay Station, late 1920s.

Even before the Shrewsbury & Birmingham Railway had won Parliament's consent for its branch to Coalbrookdale, the Wellington & Severn Junction Railway had been given permission during the summer of 1853 to build its own line from Wellington to Lightmoor. Work began in 1855 under the guidance of the much-in-demand Henry Robertson - he had acted as engineer to all three of 'The Fighting Shrewsburys' and would also serve as Shrewsbury's MP on three occasions. The line was completed and opened as far as Horsehay & Dawley on 15 May 1857.

In the following spring the line had reached Lightmoor although initially only goods trains worked the route. However, in August 1861 a passenger service was introduced and eventually worked as far as Coalbrookdale via Lightmoor (from where services could also reverse backwards onto the former Shrewsbury & Birmingham main line at Shifnal). That same year the line was leased jointly to the Great Western Railway and the West Midland Railway. The latter had been established in 1860 following the merger of three smaller companies and was closely allied to the Great Western in order to fend off the attentions of the London & North Western. Horsehay soon emerged as the largest and most important intermediate stop along the branch, with a bustling freight yard serving numerous pits and ironworks nearby. Milk traffic also generated much revenue as did the carrying of pigeons.

Meanwhile, to the south-west of Coalbrookdale, across the River Severn, the Much Wenlock & Severn Junction Railway developed its own 3-mile line from the town of Much Wenlock to Buildwas. This opened on 1 February 1862 for passenger services and it was perhaps inevitable that it would quickly become joined to the Wellington & Severn Junction Railway across the river. This was duly achieved when the Coalbrookdale Company bridged the Severn with its Albert Edward Bridge in November 1864. As a result through services from Wellington via the Wellington & Severn Junction to Much Wenlock (over Much Wenlock & Severn Junction tracks) soon appeared.

The next logical step was to create a 14-mile link from Much Wenlock to Craven Arms on the Shrewsbury & Hereford Railway's main line. This would then allow for a direct service from Wellington to deep within the adjoining county of Herefordshire and on into South Wales.

Longville Station.

However, building this additional line, which was the responsibility of the Much Wenlock, Craven Arms & Coalbrookdale Railway (more commonly known as the Wenlock Railway), took over six years to complete because of stubborn opposition to the chosen route by a handful of local landowners. So strong was this resistance that after time the original route of the railway was altered through the addition of an expensive tunnel near Presthope. Building this piece of major civil engineering severely delayed progress on completing the rest of the line.

However, by December 1864 much of the branch had opened for business and the rest, from Presthope to Marsh Farm Junction on the Shrewsbury & Hereford Railway near Craven Arms, was ready three years later. To cater for the increased number of trains passing through its vicinity, the station at Much Wenlock was considerably upgraded with a new building, extra sidings and a goods depot.

The full 28 miles of track stretching from Ketley Junction to Marsh Farm later became considered as one complete route, even though it was in reality comprised of three individual (but connecting) lines. It was also one of the most scenic anywhere in Britain. In the fullness of time it passed into the ownership of the Great Western and, in a bid to fend off the growing threat posed by motor buses, the new owner opened several small halts during the 1930s to lure more passengers.

Rushbury Station, 1932.

In the Second World War the line enjoyed a considerable boom as it was heavily utilised by fuel trains serving a large underground gasoline storage dump which the military had built near Farley Halt. When peace returned in 1945 the line slipped back into decline as increasing numbers of people opted to use road rather than rail transport. This drop in numbers was most noticeable along the Much Wenlock—Craven Arms stretch and this was the first to see passenger trains withdrawn in December 1951. The remainder of the line up to Wellington carried on for a further eleven years before it too closed on 23 July 1962.

Nowadays the Telford Horsehay Steam Trust preservation group has its headquarters at the former Horsehay & Dawley station. This organisation has also been responsible for restoring a section of the line from Horsehay Yard to Doseley Halt and it has current plans to extend the restoration further with Lightmoor or beyond as the objective.

Oswestry—Welshpool

Passenger service withdrawn	18 January 1965	*Stations closed*	*Date*
Distance	16 miles	Llanymynech	18 January 1965
Company	Oswestry & Newtown Railway	Four Crosses	18 January 1965
		Pool Quay	18 January 1965
Stations closed	*Date*	Buttington **	12 September 1960
Oswestry (Cam)	7 November 1966		
Llynclys	18 January 1965	* Originally known as Pant until July 1924.	
Pant (Salop) *	18 January 1965	** Originally known as Cefn Junction.	

Oswestry Station.

In June 1855 the Oswestry & Newtown Railway sought Parliamentary approval to build a railway between Oswestry in Shropshire across the border to Welshpool in Wales. Work on the line began two years later and in May 1860 the Oswestry & Newtown began running passenger trains as far as Pool Quay, followed three months later by a full service along the entire branch.

During 1862 the line was doubled between Buttington and Welshpool, as was the section from Oswestry to Llanymynech in 1864. That year the Oswestry & Newtown joined forces with the Llanidloes & Newtown, Newtown & Machynlleth and the Oswestry, Ellesmere & Whitchurch Railways to form the Cambrian Railways organisation. This new company later went on to become the largest independent Welsh railway, yet somewhat surprisingly it chose to establish its head offices in the English town of Oswestry. As a result the once small Shropshire town grew in size and became rail dominated with extensive locomotive works, sidings and engine sheds. It also featured two stations - the former Oswestry & Newtown site which the Cambrian took over and referred to as Oswestry (Cam), plus the old Shrewsbury & Chester facility which had passed into the hands of the Great Western Railway during 1854.

Llanymynech Station.

After the 1923 Groupings the Cambrian lost its independence and was absorbed by the enlarged Great Western. The two stations in Oswestry therefore became unnecessary and in July 1924 the original Great Western stop was converted into a goods depot, allowing Oswestry (Cam) to be extended so that it could accommodate all trains calling at the town.

The Oswestry—Welshpool line survived into nationalisation and the British Railways era, by which time competition from local bus operators was beginning to bite. Falling passenger numbers ensued which, combined with the higher operating costs involved in running a train service and the growing willingness of nearby freight hauliers to switch to road transport, all conspired to blight the line's profitability. Thus in January 1965 British Railways terminated all passenger services along the branch.

Oswestry (Cam) survived the withdrawal of these trains for a short time by handling local services to Gobowen but eventually closed in late 1966. Welshpool however remained open as it was still being used by trains out of Shrewsbury which arrived via the old junction at Buttington (see the next section).

A stretch of the branch has been acquired from Llynclys to Pant by the Cambrian Railways Trust Preservation Society. After sufficient funds had been obtained the Trust relaid much of the former track between these two sites and introduced plans to run a small shuttle service using a restored diesel multiple unit.

Shrewsbury—Minsterley Branch

Passenger service withdrawn	5 February 1951
Distance	9 miles
Company	Shrewsbury & Welshpool Railway

Stations closed	*Date*
Hanwood	12 September 1960
Plealey Road	5 February 1951
Pontesbury	5 February 1951
Minsterley Ticket Platform	5 February 1951
Minsterley	5 February 1951

Plealey Road Station, April 1966.

Minsterley Station.

This branch opened in February 1861 and the following year a connection was added near Hanwood to connect with the Oswestry & Newtown Railway's branch to Welshpool at Buttington, thus giving travellers from Shrewsbury a means of reaching Welshpool or beyond by train. After four years of operations the Shrewsbury & Welshpool Railway was vested jointly by the Great Western Railway and the London & North Western Railway, but despite this passenger numbers remained disappointingly low.

By the beginning of the 1900s the branch provided seven trains in each direction every day along with a single Sunday service. On average the trip to Minsterley took half an hour to complete, much of it passing through the beautiful landscape of the Rea Brook Valley and, as well as people, the line carried milk, local agricultural produce, and a sizeable volume of mineral goods from the nearby Stiperstones mining area. Much of the latter was transferred to the branch at Pontesbury from the Snailbeach District Railway, which opened in 1877 specifically to serve the mining (and later quarrying) businesses around the Stiperstones.

After the First World War a motor bus service was introduced between Shrewsbury and Minsterley. This had a serious impact upon the line's revenue, forcing various economy measures to be initiated including the use of mixed passenger-freight trains. After the 1923 Groupings the branch became a joint venture between the Great Western and the London, Midland & Scottish Railway.

Passenger figures increased during the Second World War as a result of severe petrol rationing but dropped away again after 1945. In February 1951 British Railways withdrew all passenger services with the stops along the branch closing, although the line itself remained opened for through services into Wales and goods traffic using the former junction at Buttington.

The Coalport (East) Branch

Passenger service withdrawn	2 June 1952	*Stations closed*	*Date*
Distance	8 miles	Dawley & Stirchley	2 June 1952
Company	London & North Western Railway	Madeley Market	2 June 1952
		Coalport (East) ***	2 June 1952
Stations closed	*Date*		
Hadley	7 September 1964	* Originally known as Oakengates until June 1951.	
Oakengates Market Street *	2 June 1952	** This station was first closed between January 1917 and February 1919.	
Malins Lee **	2 June 1952	*** Originally known as Coalport (L&NW) when opened.	

Oakengates Market Street Station, 1932.

After establishing itself at Wellington in 1847 following its leasing of the Shropshire Union Railway & Canal Company's line to Stafford, the London & North Western sought to challenge the supremacy of the Great Western's links to the industrialised area covering Madeley, Coalbrookdale and Coalport. Whereas the Great Western already had rail access to a number of mines and ironworks in this area, the London & North Western had only the Shropshire Canal (an independent branch of the Shropshire Union Canal it had inherited from the Shropshire Union Railways & Canal Company) as a means of transporting goods to or from there.

This canal ran from close to the village of Trench down to Coalport on the River Severn and served the pits and ironworks of the Lilleshall Company at Priorslee together with the Court foundries at Madeley. The blast furnaces near Coalport, the ironworks of Horsehay and the Coalbrookdale Company's works at Coalbrookdale itself were also ministered to. Such important trade could not be ignored but the canal suffered terribly from subsidence and an almost permanent shortage of water. With the Great Western hovering in the wings the London & North Western was forced to act.

Malins Lee Station, 1932.

However, faced with a hefty repair bill just to keep the Shropshire Canal functioning as it was, the company proposed closing it and converting several stretches into a single-track railway which was to run from Hadley Junction on the Shropshire Union Railways & Canal Company's line to Stafford. The scheme was first suggested in 1855 (two years after an earlier London & North Western idea to create a line from Wellington to Coalport and Ironbridge had been rejected by Parliament) and after two years of debate the MPs at Westminster finally gave their consent. Work began almost immediately with the railway following the line of the Shropshire Canal to a point east of the village of Dawley before making its own way southwards to Brookside and Tweedale then on to Coalport.

Coalport Station, from the buffer stops, 1932.

The branch opened on 17 June 1861 and eight months later the Great Western also reached Coalport with its own line and built a rival station directly across the Severn from the London & North Western terminus. Not surprisingly this caused a degree of confusion and eventually the London & North Western opted to change the name of its station to Coalport (East). However, this move did nothing to bolster passenger numbers along the line as it transpired that a journey from Wellington to Coalport (East) took more than half an hour to complete despite the branch only being 8 miles long. This was because of the rural nature of the route which limited train speeds and the number of intermediate stops the London & North Western had opened up along the way. Not unsurprisingly the stop-start nature of trains using the line soon led to them being derisively nicknamed 'Coalport Dodgers'. Freight services, however, did much better thanks to the line's close proximity to the surrounding coal mines and ironworks.

After 1923 the branch passed to the LMS before becoming part of the nationalised British Railways in 1948. Road competition by this time was seriously beginning to erode much of the line's business and on 2 June 1952 all passenger services were withdrawn. Goods services continued and carried on using the line for a dozen more years before it was closed completely.

Woofferton—Tenbury Wells Branch

Passenger service withdrawn	31 July 1961
Distance	5 miles
Company	Tenbury Railway

Stations closed	*Date*
Woofferton	31 July 1961
Easton Court *	31 July 1961
Tenbury Wells **	1 August 1962

* Sometimes referred to as 'Easton Court for Little Hereford'
and first closed between October 1862 and April 1865.
** Originally known as Tenbury until November 1912.

Woofferton Station, early 1920s.

In an effort to provide a freight route from the Midlands to the River Severn the Kington, Leominster & Stourport Canal (more commonly known as the Leominster Canal) was planned. However, only 18 miles of this ambitious waterway was ever built and it struggled to survive before being sold off to the Shrewsbury & Hereford Railway whereupon closure followed during 1859. That same year, with the support of the S&H which provided some of the necessary land by offering up stretches of the Leominster Canal, the Tenbury Railway was established to build a single-track branch from Woofferton (on the Shrewsbury & Hereford's main line) to the spa town of Tenbury Wells.

Tenbury Wells Station.

The line duly opened on 1 August 1861 and the following year services began to be operated by the Great Western following its joint leasing of the Shrewsbury & Hereford with the London & North Western. There was one intermediate stop along the line at Easton Court but this closed a year after opening only to be restored to use three years later in the spring of 1865.

Tenbury Wells attracted many visitors because of its saline springs which were popular during the Victorian Age as a treatment for many skin conditions or other maladies. The Tenbury Railway's station here was actually built about half a mile from the town itself, at Burford, where one of the local landowners, Lord Northwick, resided. The facilities soon included two platforms, a pair of signal boxes (one of which closed in the 1920s), various sidings and even a locomotive turntable.

It took on average just 12 minutes to travel along the length of the line and during its time a variety of locomotives and rolling stock were employed. In later years Great Western-designed diesel railcars were also introduced to improve efficiency and lower operating costs. Britain's railways were nationalised in 1948 to become British Railways and, while the branch survived to see this historic event, as was so often the case the boom in road transport led to the withdrawal of its passenger timetable in July 1961.

The Severn Valley Line

Passenger service withdrawn	9 September 1963	*Stations closed*	*Date*
Distance	40 miles	Rifle Range Halt	4 October 1920
Company	Severn Valley Railway	Foley Park †	5 January 1970
		Bewdley	5 January 1970
Stations closed	*Date*	Burlish ††	5 January 1970
Berrington	9 September 1963	Stourport-on-Severn †††	5 January 1970
Cound Halt	9 September 1963		
Cressage	9 September 1963	* Originally known as Ironbridge & Broseley until November 1895.
Buildwas	9 September 1963	** Original station closed 1 March 1954 and replaced by a new structure
Iron Bridge & Broseley *	9 September 1963	360 metres further south.
Jackfield Halt **	9 September 1963	*** Originally known as Coalport.
Coalport West ***	9 September 1963	**** Originally known as Linley until 10 September 1951.
Linley Halt ****	9 September 1963	***** Originally known as Alveley Colliery Sidings until June 1954.
Bridgnorth	9 September 1963	† Originally known as Foley Park Halt until May 1968.
Eardington	9 September 1963	†† Originally known as Burlish Halt until May 1968.
Alveley Halt *****	9 September 1963	††† Originally known as Stourport until October 1934.

Linley Halt.

Eardington Station.

The original Severn Valley Railway's (SVR) approach to Parliament for approval of its plan to build a line linking Shrewsbury to Worcester was made in 1853. The scheme, which was readily accepted, not only foresaw the railway as improving communications between the county capitals of Shropshire and Worcestershire but also as a means of providing transportation for a number of agricultural and industrial areas in the process.

However, it took nine years to build the Severn Valley Railway which was single-tracked throughout its length and generally followed the course of the River Severn. As a consequence the line became notable for its many gradients (reaching 1 in 100 at some spots), numerous viaducts and several tunnels including one of close to 600 yards length at Bridgnorth. Thirteen intermediate stations were also provided most of which featured two platforms and a passing loop.

The line opened for passenger trains on 1 February 1862, with the West Midland Railway providing the locomotives and rolling stock. In the beginning a timetable of four trains each way, every day, between Shrewsbury and Bridgnorth was provided with additional workings to Hartlebury which acted as a junction with the West Midland's Kidderminster to Worcester line. There were additional benefits to be gained from moving coal and local farm produce while at Buildwas a link to Much Wenlock was available on the Wellington—Craven Arms line. As a result of this Buildwas grew in importance as a busy junction station.

Bewdley Station, c. 1915.

The West Midland amalgamated with the Great Western in 1863 and nine years later the Severn Valley Railway itself was formally absorbed into 'God's Wonderful Railway' (the Great Western's nickname) as it continued to grow and strengthen its position across western England. During 1878 the Great Western improved the Severn Valley line by opening up a connection from Bewdley (where there was a junction to the Tenbury line) to Kidderminster. This enabled services from Birmingham to reach the Severn Valley directly.

Despite such measures passenger revenues remained poor and the importance of freight grew significantly. During the 1930s, in a bid to boost passenger interest, the Great Western opened up several new halts and laid on diesel railcars for many services but with little discernible results. However, during the Second World War the line benefited greatly from the creation of a Royal Air Force base close to Bridgnorth. This meant that a large number of service personnel arrived or departed by train but the upturn was all too brief.

Once peace returned so did the line's downward trend. Growing road competition cut profit levels even further and it was left to the nationalised British Railways to deliver the knockout punch. On 9 September 1963 all passenger trains working between Shrewsbury and Bewdley via the Severn Valley were withdrawn. This was followed by the termination of freight trains over the same stretch six years later.

The Severn Valley Line

Stourport Station, *c.* 1912.

However, passenger trains were still operating from Kidderminster via Bewdley to Stourport and Hartlebury. These took the form of a regular shuttle service and when British Rail (as British Railways had been rebranded in 1965) announced plans to close this stretch of line there was a considerable public outcry. As a result BR was forced to postpone its original closure date from April 1969 until 3 January 1970 with the affected stations closing their doors two days later.

The Severn Valley was far from dead though. In 1965 the Severn Valley Railway Society had been formed by a group of volunteers to preserve a portion of the line in full working order. Today, the society operates the largest fleet of historic locomotives and rolling stock anywhere in Britain and continues to provide 'real' trains for the public to use and enjoy on regular services between Kidderminster Town station (which was purpose built especially for the society) via Eardington to Bridgnorth. These two stations were reopened by the society (although Eardington was closed again in 1983) along with the stops at Highley, Arley, Northwood and Bewdley, thus keeping much of the old line in use.

Oswestry—Whitchurch Branch

Passenger service withdrawn	18 January 1965
Distance	22 miles
Company	Oswestry, Ellesmere & Whitchurch Railway

Stations closed	*Date*
Tinkers Green Halt	18 January 1965
Whittington High Level *	4 January 1960
Frankton	18 January 1965

Stations closed	*Date*
Ellesmere	18 January 1965
Welshampton	18 January 1965
Bettisfield	18 January 1965
Fenn's Bank	18 January 1965

* Originally known as Whittington (Cam) until July 1924.

Frankton Station.

The Oswestry, Ellesmere & Whitchurch Railway was planned as an important link between the London & North Western's Shrewsbury to Crewe line and for services into North Wales. The branch opened for passenger traffic on 4 May 1863 between Whitchurch and Ellesmere, with the section down to Oswestry following in July 1864. That very month the Oswestry, Ellesmere & Whitchurch Railway became one of the constituent companies that made up the Cambrian Railways.

Like many other lines in the area, the Oswestry—Whitchurch Branch passed into the hands of the Great Western after 1923 and subsequently survived to form part of British Railways twenty-five years later. Never particularly busy as a passenger line and later overshadowed by other surrounding routes, the branch fell victim to the Beeching Report and was closed to non-freight services in January 1965.

Ellesmere Station, *c.* **1910.**

Ellesmere Station, 1903.

Wellington—Market Drayton—Nantwich

Passenger service withdrawn	9 September 1963	*Stations closed*	*Date*
Distance	27 miles	Peplow	9 September 1963
Companies	Nantwich & Market Drayton Railway/	Hodnet	9 September 1963
	Wellington & Drayton Railway	Wollerton Halt	9 September 1963
		Tern Hill	9 September 1963
Stations closed	*Date*	Little Drayton Halt	6 October 1941
Longdon Halt	9 September 1963	Market Drayton	9 September 1963
Crudgington	9 September 1963	Adderley	9 September 1963
Rowton Halt	9 September 1963	Coxbank Halt	9 September 1963
Ellerdine Halt	9 September 1963		

Crudgington Station.

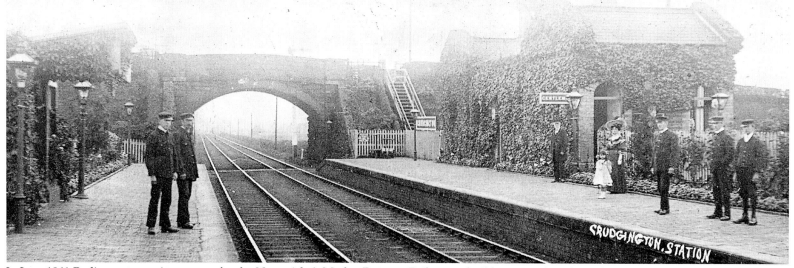

In June 1861 Parliament gave its consent for the Nantwich & Market Drayton Railway to build an 11-mile railway from Nantwich in South Cheshire to the small Shropshire town of Market Drayton. Originally there was to have been two intermediate stops along the route at Audlem in Cheshire and Adderley just across the county borderline.

The Nantwich & Market Drayton was supported by the Great Western which also backed the incorporation of the Wellington & Drayton Railway in August 1862. The Wellington & Drayton's aim was to develop a 16-mile branch between Market Drayton and Wellington on the former Shrewsbury & Birmingham main line. The Great Western was keen to promote both companies as it believed that they would allow it to gain access to the important rail junction at Crewe in Cheshire as well as Stoke-on-Trent, the centre of the Potteries industrial area of Staffordshire, thereby thwarting any similar plans by rivals such as the LNWR.

Market Drayton Station, 1911.

It was the Nantwich & Market Drayton's line which opened for business first, in October 1863, followed four years later by the Wellington & Drayton and thereby creating a through-route. Services were worked by the Great Western and in time the route became classified as a secondary main line though its stations were quite some distance apart and the passengers using them were never great in number.

Market Drayton was famous for its Wednesday street market and local bakeries. The station here was the connection point between the Nantwich & Market Drayton and the Wellington & Drayton as well as later becoming a junction point for the North Staffordshire Railway's line from Stoke-on-Trent. After Market Drayton, the last original stop before the line passed into Cheshire was Adderley, which served the nearby manor house of the same name.

Both the Nantwich & Market Drayton and the Wellington & Drayton were eventually absorbed by the Great Western in 1897. In a bid to boost passenger revenues during the 1930s the company added six small halts along the line between Wellington and Coxbank on the border with Cheshire (plus one more over it near Audlem). However, these had little effect and local services lived constantly under the threat of withdrawal long before nationalisation and the days of British Railways.

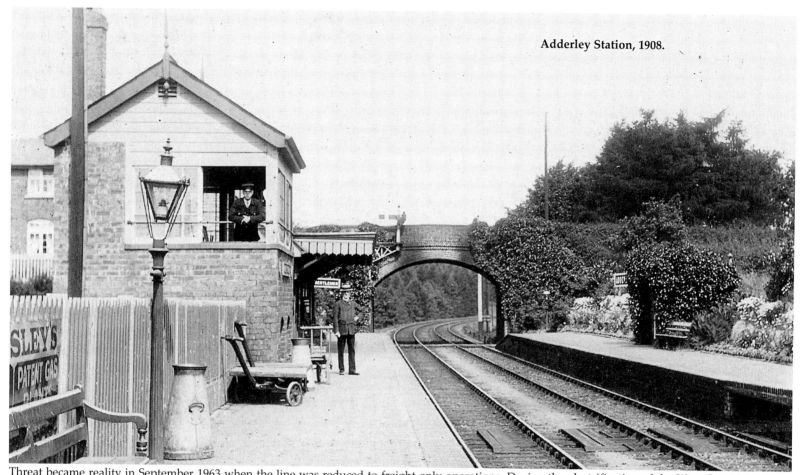

Adderley Station, 1908.

Threat became reality in September 1963 when the line was reduced to freight-only operations. During the electrification of the West Coast Main Line during the mid-1960s the line proved itself to be a useful diversionary route for London—northwest England expresses whenever engineering possessions were in force. For a brief time it appeared as if the whole line would win a reprieve after British Rail proposed opening a new marshalling yard at Walcot (between Shrewsbury and Wellington) to which it would act as an access route. However, the plan was later abandoned as the concept of block working freight trains came in to force.

Subsequently goods traffic along the line declined markedly and most of what remained was diverted to run via Stafford once the West Coast Main Line reopened. The upshot of this was that the remainder of the Wellington—Market Drayton—Nantwich line closed completely in 1967.

Tenbury—Bewdley Branch

Passenger service withdrawn	1 August 1962	*Stations closed*	*Date*
Distance	14 miles	Cleobury Mortimer	1 August 1962
Company	Tenbury & Bewdley Railway	Wyre Forest	1 August 1962

Stations closed	*Date*
Newnham Bridge *	1 August 1962
Neen Sollars **	1 August 1962

* Originally known as Newnham until May 1873.
** Originally known as Neen Sollers until 1902.

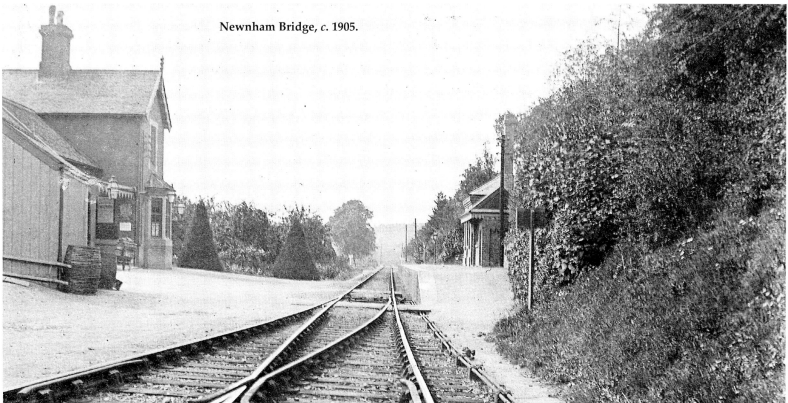

Newnham Bridge, *c.* 1905.

The station at Tenbury Wells on the Tenbury Railway line from Woofferton remained a terminus for just three years until it was reached from the east by the Tenbury & Bewdley Railway. This company, incorporated during 1860, opened for business in August 1864 and provided a link to the Severn Valley Railway with the access that line offered to Kidderminster and beyond.

Neen Sollars Station, 1953.

Trains along the branch were provided by the Great Western which eventually vested the Tenbury & Bewdley during 1869. As a general rule services ran along the line and the adjoining Woofferton—Tenbury Wells as if the two were one. Despite being a very rural concern, by the 1920s the branch had established for itself a five-trains-per-day, each-way schedule (with the exception of Sundays when no trains ran) between Woofferton and Kidderminster. During the Second World War the line also saw considerable numbers of ammunition trains traversing its length, especially around Cleobury Mortimer.

In the British Railways era, a plan to shut the branch at the same time as the Woofferton—Tenbury section caused something of a local hullabaloo and forced a rethink. To keep the branch open a reduced passenger timetable was hurriedly introduced in order to cut costs and this resulted in just a single morning train with an evening return running on weekdays only from Tenbury Wells to Bewdley.

Cleobury Mortimer Station, September 1949.

This revised operation only lasted twelve months before British Railways again raised the issue of closure. This time the suggestion became a fact and in the summer of 1962 the passenger service was officially withdrawn. Freight trains continued to ply the line, although at the start of 1964 the section between Tenbury Wells and Cleobury Mortimer was decommissioned. The remaining 6 miles to Bewdley lasted until April 1965.

The Bishop's Castle Railway

Passenger service withdrawn	20 April 1935	*Stations closed*		*Date*
Distance	9 miles	Horderley		20 April 1935
Company	Bishop's Castle Railway	Plowden		20 April 1935
		Eaton		20 April 1935
Stations closed	*Date*	Lydham Heath		20 April 1935
Stretford Bridge Junction	20 April 1935	Bishop's Castle		20 April 1935

Horderley Station.

In 1861 a private railway was authorised to provide a connection from Stretford Bridge on the Shrewsbury & Hereford's main line to the Oswestry & Newtown Railway at Montgomery in Wales via Horderley, Plowden, Eaton and Lydham Heath in Shropshire. At Lydham Heath a short branch was to be added to link the small town of Bishop's Castle.

Eaton Station.

Work on the new line began in the spring of 1863 but was soon beset by contractual disputes with the building firm and the Bishop's Castle Railway's own financial shortcomings. Eventually a new contractor was appointed and construction resumed so that by October 1865 the branch had reached Lydham Heath. The short stretch to Bishop's Castle was also completed though access to this would mean trains performing a reversing manoeuvre at Lydham Heath station.

Plowden Station.

Rather than wait for the next stretch of line into Wales to be finished, the Bishop's Castle Railway decided to open for business in February 1866. Initially, there was a regular service of four trains per day in both directions and these were usually mixed passenger-freight services hauled by the Bishop's Castle Railway's own 0-6-0 locomotive which was named 'Plowden'. Additional rolling stock was later borrowed from the Great Western Railway.

Bishop's Castle Station, May 1932.

By the close of 1866 the Bishop's Castle Railway was on the verge of bankruptcy and it's plan to build as far as Montgomery had to be shelved. When the company failed to honour its debts the bailiffs were called in and the branch was placed under the control of an official receiver. For a decade the line struggled to carry on but in early 1877 it was placed under a high court order and looked set to be permanently closed. However, in July of that year a group of local people came together and purchased the line which they then agreed to lease back to the Bishop's Castle Railway.

Train services recommenced, but it was still a struggle to make any kind of profit. Despite numerous attempts to attract outside investment and constant approaches to the Great Western Railway to take charge, nobody seemed interested in the line. Even after the groupings of 1923 the Bishop's Castle Railway remained an independent concern - a fact which perhaps confirmed it had no long-term future, especially in light of growing road competition. This proved to be so for in April 1935 passenger services were withdrawn and the entire branch closed down.

'The Potts' Line'

Stations closed	Date
Passenger service withdrawn	6 November 1933
Distance	31 miles
Company	Potteries, Shrewsbury & North Wales Railway

Stations closed	*Date*
Shrewsbury Abbey *	29 February 1960
Hookagate and Redhill**	6 November 1933
Edgebold ***	6 November 1933
Cruckton	6 November 1933
Shoot Hill	6 November 1933
Ford Halt (military only)	29 February 1960
Ford & Crossgates ****	6 November 1933
Shrawardine Halt (military only)	29 February 1960
Shrawardine *****	6 November 1933
Nesscliff Halt (military only)	29 February 1960
Nesscliff & Pentre †	6 November 1933
Pentre Halt (military only)	29 February 1960
Edgerley Halt	6 November 1933
Kinnerley Halt (military only)	29 February 1960
Kinnerley Junction ††	6 November 1933
Wern Las	6 November 1933
Maesbrook †††	6 November 1933
Llanymynech Junction ††††	29 February 1960

* First closed between December 1866 and December 1868 and then between June 1880 and April 1911. Closed again between November 1933 and June 1941 when it was reopened by the War Department.

** Originally known as Red Hill until May 1921 then renamed as Hookagate until 1927.

*** Originally known as Hanwood Road until April 1921. First closed between December 1866 and December 1868 and then between June 1880 and April 1911.

**** Original station closed in December 1866. Reopened as Ford & Cross Gates in December 1868; renamed as Ford & Crossgates in April 1911.

***** First closed between December 1866 and December 1868 and then between June 1880 and April 1911.

† Originally known as Nesscliff until June 1913. First closed between December 1866 and December 1868 and then between June 1880 and June 1913.

†† Originally known as Kinnerley until April 1911. First closed between December 1866 and December 1868 and then between June 1880 and April 1911.

††† First closed between December 1866 and December 1868 and then between June 1880 and April 1911.

†††† First closed between June 1880 and April 1911 and then between November 1933 and June 1941 when it was reopened by the War Department.

Originally conceived by the West Shropshire Mineral Railway and subsequently adopted by the Shrewsbury & North Wales Railway, this branch was planned to diverge from the Shrewsbury to Welshpool (via Buttington) line just south of Shrewsbury to reach Llanymynech on the Welsh border. However, for a time the scheme remained in limbo until, somewhat surprisingly, the North Staffordshire Railway threw its weight behind the idea as a means of extending its influence across Shropshire. Thanks to the North Staffordshire the Potteries, Shrewsbury & North Wales Railway came into being and the line, which was primarily intended to carry passengers, moved a step closer to reality.

Originally the Potteries, Shrewsbury & North Wales Railway wanted to run services in and out of Shrewsbury's existing station, but this was vetoed by Parliament and so a new stop had to be built at Shrewsbury Abbey, complete with independent approach lines, storage sidings and yard. In August 1866 the branch formally opened and soon became known as 'The 'Potts' Line' - an abbreviation of its official title.

It was not long before the Potteries, Shrewsbury & North Wales ran into financial problems and at the end of 1866 the bailiffs moved in to seize control. A rescue plan involving a merger with several small Welsh railways failed to materialise, but in December 1868 services were resumed at a reduced level after the line's operating costs had been lowered by reducing it to single-track status.

The Potteries, Shrewsbury & North Wales's monetary hardships refused to go away and in 1880 all services were again suspended. This time the line remained closed until the spring of 1911 when trains started running again under the control of the Shropshire & Montgomery Light Railway. This company obtained a light railway order for the line and rebuilt much of its decayed infrastructure under the guidance of the noted proponent of light railways, Colonel H.F. Stephens.

Shrewsbury Abbey Foregate Platform.

Despite this passenger numbers remained disheartening and by the 1920s the Shropshire & Montgomery Light Railway had been forced to introduce a number of economies in order to save money. These included the use of Ford railcars (nicknamed 'Rattlers' due to the noise their wheels made) and an ex-London County Council tramcar. This particular piece had previously been a horse-drawn, double-decker carriage but Colonel Stephens had its top floor removed, along with access stairs, and railway axles were added to convert it into an unorthodox passenger coach. This was then hauled along the line behind a second-hand light engine named 'Gazelle' which had been working 'The Potts' Line' since 1911.

Shrawardine Station, 1911.

After the Colonel passed away in 1931 the condition of the branch declined sharply and in November 1933 the Shropshire & Montgomery Light Railway withdrew all passenger services bar the occasional excursion trip. Slowly the line (which had always been prone to flooding) decayed and its future looked bleak.

Kinnerley Junction Station.

Then, during the Second World War, the entire branch was taken over by the War Department in order to supply the large number of ammunition dumps and supply depots that had sprung up across this part of Shropshire. After the war the military retained control of the line until the end of 1959, by which time most of the nearby bases and depots had been closed down. The following year British Railways assumed control but the line's lack of business now that the military had gone meant it was ripe for closure, which duly occurred on 29 February 1960.

Maesbrook Station, 1903.

Kinnerley Criggion Branch

Passenger service withdrawn	6 November 1933	*Stations closed*		*Date*
Distance	6 miles	Llandrino Road *		30 October 1932
Company	Potteries, Shrewsbury & North Wales Railway	Criggion *		30 October 1932

Stations closed	*Date*
Chapel Lane	6 November 1933
Melverley *	6 November 1933
Crew Green **	30 October 1932

* First closed between June 1880 and July 1912.
** Originally known as Crewe Green until September 1920 and first closed between June 1880 and July 1912.

As part of the Potteries, Shrewsbury & North Wales Railway's incorporation the company was required to build a 6-mile long branch line off 'The Potts' Line' from Kinnerley Junction to the granite quarries at Criggion just across the Welsh border. A secondary passenger service was also to be provided for which a handful of new stations were to be built.

The branch was duly completed and opened in June 1871 after the Potteries, Shrewsbury & North Wales's first spell of financial difficulty. Except at Melverley (where a wooden viaduct carried the track across the River Severn), all of the line's stops were built out of wood to save money and lacked even the most basic facilities.

Like 'The Potts' Line', the Kinnerley Criggion branch struggled to generate much passenger interest although it did do rather better in terms of freight movement, especially stone. However, when the Potteries, Shrewsbury & North Wales collapsed for a second time in 1880 the branch's activities were suspended.

Melverley Station, September 1958.

Due to this inactivity much of the line's infrastructure deteriorated over time and in 1902 the viaduct at Melverley suddenly collapsed into the Severn, forcing repairs to be conducted at considerable expense. In February 1912 the Shropshire & Montgomery Light Railway took charge and a passenger timetable was reintroduced six months later.

Nevertheless, by 1932 the line was again in trouble with the Melverley Viaduct again proving the source of most difficulties. Judged to be unsafe, the bridge was taken out of use for passenger trains and henceforth such trains terminated at Melverley. The Shropshire & Montgomery Light Railway eventually paid to have the bridge repaired but in November 1933 the company decided to cut its losses and withdrew a passenger service altogether, leaving the line open only for goods traffic which lasted until 1959 when the branch closed as road transportation took over. The troublesome Melverley Viaduct was eventually (and somewhat ironically) rebuilt as a more substantial road bridge.

Cleobury Mortimer—Ditton Priors Branch

Passenger service withdrawn	26 September 1938	*Stations closed*	*Date*
Distance	12 miles	Aston Botterell Siding	26 September 1938
Company	Cleobury Mortimer & Ditton Priors Light Railway	Burwarton Halt ***	26 September 1938
		Cleobury North Crossing	26 September 1938
Stations closed	*Date*	Ditton Priors Halt ****	26 September 1938
Cleobury Town Halt *	26 September 1938		
Chilton Halt	1 June 1917	* Originally known as Cleobury Town until October 1923.
Detton Ford Siding	26 September 1938	** Originally known as Stottesdon until October 1923.
Prescott Siding	26 September 1938	*** Originally known as Burwarton until October 1923.
Stottesdon Halt **	26 September 1938	**** Originally known as Ditton Priors until October 1923.

This branch line was unusual in that it changed hands four times during its lifespan. Originally the line was proposed under a Light Railway Order of March 1901 as the Cleobury Mortimer & Ditton Priors Light Railway. The objective was to build a line from Cleobury Mortimer (on the Tenbury—Bewdley branch) to a terminus at Ditton Priors close to where several quarrying firms were operating in the nearby Clee Hills. Primarily the line was viewed as a freight concern, although a secondary passenger service was also considered from the outset.

The line duly opened for freight in July 1908 (the lengthy construction time being a result of the company's financial problems) and a passenger timetable began four months later. Initially two mixed freight/passenger trains operated each way on certain weekdays using only a pair of Manning Wardle 0-6-0ST locomotives and a quartet of four-wheeled carriages.

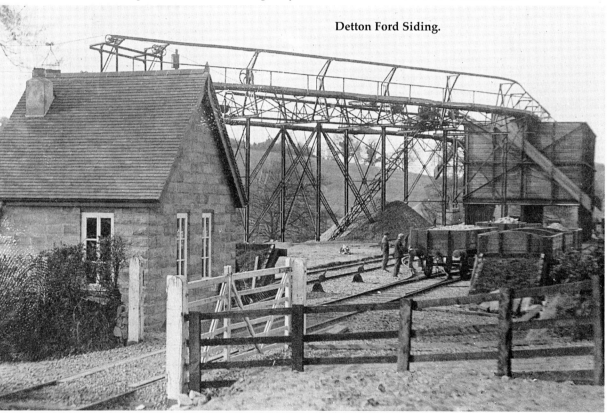

Detton Ford Siding.

Ditton Priors Station.

By 1910 the Cleobury Mortimer & Ditton Priors Light Railway was carrying 15,000 passengers and more than 75,000 tons of cargo annually. As a result several expansion schemes were considered, but none ever saw the light of day and in the years running up to the outbreak of the First World War the company saw its passenger revenues decline due to the remoteness of the line and the advent of the first motor buses. Freight was still doing well though and in May 1922 the company was officially absorbed by the Great Western Railway as a profitable enterprise.

Passenger figures continued to fall and by the early 1930s even the traditional movement of stone was in jeopardy as the local quarries became exhausted. After persevering for as long as it could afford to do so the Great Western announced the withdrawal of all passenger trains from the branch on 26 September 1938, despite a local campaign to keep the timetable running.

When the Second World War erupted the line was considered useful because the redundant quarries provided useful areas for storing military ammunition and explosives. Overnight the branch became a hive of activity once more and remained that way until peace returned in 1945.

Thereafter, a tortuous decline set in which continued throughout British Railways stewardship. Then, in May 1957, the Admiralty took control as it maintained an ammunition depot nearby at Ditton Priors and needed the line for access. Under the new ownership the branch saw 0-4-0 diesel shunters working most trains.

When the Tenbury—Bewdley line ceased operating a passenger service in 1962 the future of the branch to Ditton Priors was put under the spotlight once again. Not unexpectedly, closure soon followed with the branch being formally decommissioned on 16 April 1965.

Closed stations on lines still open to passenger traffic

Shrewsbury—Welshpool

Stations closed	Date
Shrewsbury West	6 November 1933
Meole Brace	6 November 1933
Yockleton Halt	12 September 1960
Westbury	12 September 1960
Plas-Y-Court Halt	12 September 1960
Breidden	12 September 1960

Shrewsbury—Wolverhampton

Stations closed	Date
Abbey Foregate Platform	30 September 1912
Upton Magna	7 September 1964
Walcot	7 September 1964
Admaston Halt	7 September 1964
New Hadley	11 May 1985

Yockleton Station, *c.* **1910.**

Shrewsbury—Wrexham

Stations closed	Date
Leaton	12 September 1960
Oldwoods Halt	12 September 1960
Baschurch	12 September 1960
Stanwardine Halt	12 September 1960
Haughton Halt	12 September 1960
Rednal & West Felton	12 September 1960
Whittington Low Level	12 September 1960
Weston Rhyn	12 September 1960
Trehowell Halt	29 October 1951

Shrewsbury—Hereford

Stations closed	Date
Shrewsbury English Bridge	31 May 1899
Condover	9 June 1958
Dorrington	9 June 1958
Leebotwood	9 June 1958
Little Stretton Halt	9 June 1958
Marsh Brook	9 June 1958
Onibury	9 June 1958
Bromfield	9 June 1958
Ashford Bowdler	1 November 1855

Leaton Station, 1910.